D0996468

First published 2020 by The O'Brien Press Ltd,
12 Terenure Road East, Rathgar, Dublin 6, D06 HD27, Ireland.
Tel: +353 1 4923333; Fax: +353 1 4922777
E-mail: books@obrien.ie
Website: www.obrien.ie
The O'Brien Press is a member of Publishing Ireland.

ISBN: 978-1-78849-166-2

Cover Design: Emma Byrne
Cover image: Shutterstock

7 6 5 4 3 2 1
24 23 22 21 20

Printed and bound by Gutenberg Press, Malta.
The paper used in this book is produced using pulp from
managed forests.

Published in:

DUBLIN
UNESCO
City of Literature

# Symbols

*of*

# Ireland

Eoin O'Brien

THE O'BRIEN PRESS

DUBLIN

Sin — ne Fian-na Fáil

**'Amhrán na bhFiann'**

'Amhrán na bhFiann' ('The Soldier's Song') is the national anthem of Ireland. Written around 1910 and sung during the 1916 Rising, it became our official anthem in 1926. Unusually for a national anthem, the lyrics are very warlike, a cry for independence and freedom from a foreign enemy.

## Aran jumper

Originating in the Aran Islands in Galway Bay, Aran knitting can be found right down the west coast. The patterns are thought to have been inspired by Celtic knotwork. Aran garments are hugely popular worldwide, and in 2017, the Aran jumper was chosen as one of the world's most iconic fashion items.

## The Ardagh Chalice

Found in 1868 by two young men digging up potatoes in County Limerick, this is one of the greatest treasures of the early Irish Christian Church, dating from the eighth century. It includes incredibly intricate spiral and interlacing patterns in gold filigree. The Sam Maguire Cup, presented each year to the winners of the All-Ireland Gaelic football final, is modelled on the Ardagh Chalice.

## Banshee

If you hear a mournful wail out in the dark in the night, it could be a banshee, warning you that a member of your family is soon to die. A banshee usually looks like an old woman, dressed in a grey robe, with pale skin and red eyes from constant crying.

## Blarney

According to one Irish politician, blarney is 'flattery sweetened by humour and flavoured by wit'. The name comes from a large stone set into the wall of Blarney Castle in County Cork. You simply have to dangle backwards and upside-down at a dizzying height and kiss the stone to win the 'gift of the gab'.

## Bodhrán

The bodhrán is Ireland's traditional drum, made of a wooden surround with treated goatskin stretched across it. It is held under the arm, with one hand against the inside of the skin, while the other hand plays it with a two-ended beater. It's possible to play very sophisticated rhythms on this pretty basic instrument.

### The Book of Kells

Regarded by many as the most beautiful book in the world, and probably Ireland's greatest national treasure, this is a copy of the four gospels written in Latin and dating from around AD 800. Named after Kells Monastery, County Meath, where it was hidden for many years, it is now housed in the Old Library in Trinity College, Dublin.

## Brian Ború

Brian was born in County Clare around AD 941, a son of the King of Thomond. At that time, Ireland was ruled by 150 regional kings, all squabbling and raiding cattle from one another. Viking raids were also frequent. Brian gradually established control over the whole country and, in 1011, became High King of Ireland. He is best known for his victory at the Battle of Clontarf on 23 April 1014, securing Irish unity, though he was killed in the battle's aftermath.

### Cathleen Ní Houlihan

Also known as Dark Rosaleen and the *sean-bhean bhocht* (pronounced 'shan-van vukt', 'the poor old woman'), this is a nationalist symbol, the spirit of Ireland represented as a woman. She has featured in many songs, poems and plays down through the centuries.

## Celtic cross

The Celtic form of the Christian cross features a ring, or nimbus, encircling the middle of the cross. Its meaning is unclear, but it may represent the sun. There are enormous and ancient Celtic 'high crosses' all over the country, such as at Monasterboice, Clonmacnoise and Glendalough, many with biblical scenes carved into them.

Marino Branch
Brainse Marino
Tel: 8336297

## Claddagh ring

This 'fede' (faith) ring originated in the small fishing village of Claddagh, now part of Galway city. Designed by silversmiths in the seventeenth century, the Claddagh ring features a heart, wearing a crown, held by the thumbs and fingertips of two hands. The heart represents love; the crown, loyalty; and the hands, friendship.

## Connemara pony

A tough and hardy breed originating in the wild and rugged region of Connemara in west County Galway, Connemara ponies are great for all sorts of sports and are famously gentle with children. Thought to be a mix of early Viking ponies and horses brought over by the Spanish Armada around 1600, they are now popular all over the world.

## Cows

Ireland, of course, has the best milk, cream, butter and beef in the world, as our cattle are fed almost entirely on the grass that grows so abundantly here. Though calm and docile, cows are also playful and curious and will wander over to greet you, especially if you sing to them.

## Craic

The concept of 'craic' can be difficult to explain – somewhere between fun, chat and humour. It's what is happening when you look across the table and see mischievous grins spreading across faces, or hear songs spontaneously starting up, and you can't help but erupt into bellowing laughter.

## Croke Park

The third-largest stadium in Europe, with seats for 82,300 people, 'Croker' is the headquarters of the Gaelic Athletic Association (GAA) and has hosted the All-Ireland hurling, camogie and Gaelic football finals since 1896. On Bloody Sunday, 21 November 1920, British troops entered the ground and fired into the crowd, killing fourteen. Many concerts have also taken place in the stadium over the years.

## Cúchulainn

Born Setanta, son of the god Lugh, he earned the name Cúchulainn – the hound of Culann – when as a child he killed a ferocious war hound with his hurley and sliotar. One of Ireland's greatest mythical heroes, Cúchulainn famously held back the entire army of Connacht singlehandedly, in the epic saga *The Táin*.

### Cup of tea

Of course, there is nothing more Irish than a cup of tea. However hard you've been working, however far you've travelled, whatever worries might be on your mind, or whatever earth-shattering piece of news you're bursting to share or discuss, a nice cup of tea will sort it all out.

## Currach

This style of boat is found only on the west coast of Ireland. With a frame of wooden ribs, over which tarred canvas (or in times past, animal hide) is stretched, it is very lightweight and highly manoeuvrable. Powered by oars, until recently it was the main form of transport to and from Ireland's western islands, and was used for fishing out on the Atlantic.

### Dolmen

A dolmen, or *cromlech*, is a type of ancient tomb consisting of several vertical megaliths holding up a colossal, flat topstone, weighing up to a hundred tons. Dating from around 4000 to 3000 BC, about 190 of them can be found in Ireland, including the iconic Poulnabrone in Clare and the huge Brownshill dolmen in Carlow. Many dolmens were originally covered with a mound of stones and earth.

## Donkey

Donkeys are fantastically friendly creatures, great as pets as well as powerful working animals. They have long been an integral part of Irish country life, used for transport, carrying turf, clearing rocky fields and ploughing. They're well known for stubbornness too, but this is probably a sign that they are cleverer than horses and less willing to follow orders blindly.

### Fairy tree

A hawthorn tree standing alone in a field has always been treated with great respect, as it is believed to belong to the little people, the *sídhe* (pronounced 'shee'). It is never to be damaged or cut, as you do not want to get on the bad side of the *sídhe*.

## Flat cap

Traditionally made from tweed, woven from lamb's wool, the flat cap dates back at least 600 years and is still fashionable today. It is warm and comfortable, and the peaked front keeps the rain off and the sun out of your eyes.

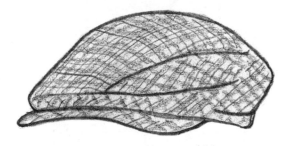

## Galway hooker

A strong, seaworthy vessel, used around Galway Bay and the west coast, the hooker has one mast, with a mainsail and two foresails. The hull is coated with pitch and so is black, while the sails are a deep red. As well as for fishing, they were traditionally used for transporting turf, cattle and other cargo. The annual festival of Cruinniú na mBád ('the gathering of the boats') involves hooker races across Galway Bay, from Connemara to Kinvara in County Galway.

## The Giant's Causeway

Near the northeastern corner of Ireland,
an ancient volcanic eruption created a
highly unusual basalt rock formation.
As the lava cooled, it fractured into
40,000 roughly hexagonal columns, up
to 40 feet (12 metres) high. Or else it is
the remains of a pathway across
to Scotland built by Irish giant
Fionn Mac Cumhaill.

## Green

Green is our national colour and the colour of the jerseys worn by our athletes in international sporting events. It is also the best colour in the world, calming and tranquil yet joyous and uplifting, the colour of life itself. According to Johnny Cash, there are 'Forty Shades of Green' to be found in Ireland.

## Guinness

Ireland's famous stout has been made at Dublin's St James's Gate brewery since 1759, and with a 9,000-year lease, that shouldn't change any time soon. The delicious smell of barley being roasted to brew Guinness regularly wafts through the city.

## Halloween

Halloween originates from the Celtic
festival of Samhain, marking the
beginning of winter. Bonfires were
lit, and it was believed to be a time
when the boundary between our world
and the Otherworld was more easily
crossed. Offerings of food and drink
were left out for the 'little people', and
the souls of the dead were thought to
revisit their old homes, looking
for hospitality.

## Harp

Ireland is the only country in the world with a musical instrument as its national symbol. Harps are mentioned in many Irish legends, and they appear on ancient stone crosses. Probably the most famous Irish harpist was the blind Turlough O'Carolan, born in 1670, thought of by many as Ireland's national composer.

## Holy well

Usually fed by underground springs,
there are hundreds of holy wells
throughout the country. They are
commonly associated with local saints,
and their waters are thought to have
curative powers for complaints such as
rheumatism, blindness or
foot problems.

## Horseshoe

Hang a horseshoe over your door, to bring you luck forever more! But make sure to hang it the right way, with the ends pointing upwards, or your luck could spill out. The lucky horseshoe may originate with the belief that some evil spirits are afraid of iron.
The luckiest horseshoes are those found by chance.

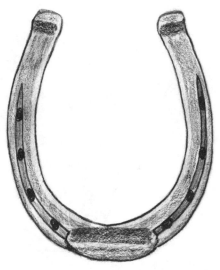

Marino Branch
Brainse Marino
Tel: 8336297

## Hurling

Hurling is Ireland's national game, and to hurl you need a hurley, also known as a hurl or, in Irish, a *camán*. You also need a *sliotar*, the ball used in hurling, traditionally made of leather. At least 3,000 years old, the game is mentioned in many Irish legends, including the story of Cúchulainn.

## Irish coffee

This combination of hot coffee, whiskey, sugar and cream was devised by chef Joe Sheridan at Foynes air base in County Limerick, in 1943. In those days, this was the landing place for flying boats, and after their long Atlantic crossing a hot pick-me-up was very welcome!

## Irish dancing

The dance most associated with Ireland is the *Riverdance* type, with the arms held down by the sides and the feet doing high kicks and high-speed steps, usually performed solo. But we also have *céilí*, performed in groups arranged in lines or a circle, and *sean nós* ('old style') dancing, which is more freeform, traditionally performed on a door laid flat or a tabletop.

### Irish elk

Long extinct, the Irish elk, *Megaloceros giganteus*, was the biggest species of deer ever to walk the Earth. Over 100 skeletons have been discovered in Ballybetagh bog in County Dublin. The Irish elk stood up to about 7 feet (2.1 metres) tall at the shoulder, with antlers up to an enormous 12 feet (3.65 metres) wide.

## Irish stew

A hearty stew, traditionally of lamb but sometimes of beef, with root vegetables, potatoes, onions, herbs and pearl barley, Irish stew will fill your belly, lift your mood and cure almost all known illnesses. It's even tastier reheated the next day.

## Irish wolfhound

These enormous dogs, the tallest of all dog breeds, are native to Ireland. Originally used for hunting, including for giant elk, boar and wolves, they were also prized for their bravery in war. They are gentle giants, though, and make fantastic pets. Legendary hero Fionn Mac Cumhaill had two favourite wolfhounds, named Bran and Sceolaing.

## Leprechaun

Usually depicted as a small, bearded man, a leprechaun is a mischievous type of fairy. If you can catch one, it will be forced to give up its treasure – a crock of gold, hidden at the end of the rainbow. Leprechauns are solitary creatures and are very skilled at leatherwork, particularly mending shoes.

## Martello tower

About fifty Martello towers were built around the coast of Ireland at the turn of the nineteenth century, to watch out for Napoleonic forces invading from France. Around 40 feet (12 metres) high, with extremely thick walls and a flat roof, they are modelled on a fort at Mortella Point in Corsica, which survived hours of sustained cannon-fire. James Joyce's *Ulysses* begins in the Martello tower in Sandycove, Dublin.

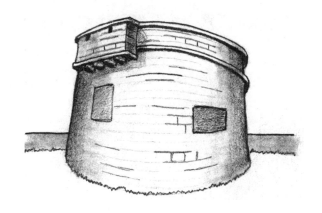

## Mary

There are many Marys in Ireland, the most famous being Mary the mother of Jesus, who is especially revered in the Irish Catholic Church. Other Marys include Robinson and McAleese, two recent presidents of the country. Nearly all of us have an Auntie Mary.

## Newgrange

This huge passage tomb in the Boyne Valley, County Meath, is 5,200 years old – older than Stonehenge or the Egyptian pyramids. At sunrise on the days around the winter solstice, 21 December, the sun's rays line up perfectly with the passage and light up the entire 62-foot (19-metre) length of the tomb. There is a lottery every year to see it!

Apple

Ash

Hazel

Holly

Oak

Scots pine

Yew

## The nobles of the wood

In ancient times, Ireland worked under a unique legal system known as *Fenechus*, or Brehon Law. The seven most valuable and useful trees were known as the 'nobles of the wood', and a heavy fine would be levied on anyone damaging them or cutting off branches. The nobles were: oak, hazel, holly, yew, ash, Scots pine and apple.

## Norman tower house

There are thousands of castles in Ireland, and the most common type is the Norman tower house. Really a fortified home, where a local lord and his family lived, it was usually three or four storeys high, with the great dining hall on the top floor. The walls are up to 4 feet (1.2 metres) thick, and there was usually a single, arched entrance, with a 'murder hole' above for pouring hot oil or shooting arrows through.

## Oak

The oak, or *daire*, has been the undisputed 'king of the forest', ever since the time of the druids. They are the biggest trees in Ireland, and the longest-lived, with a lifespan of 900 years. To the Celts, the oak represented truth, courage and wisdom.

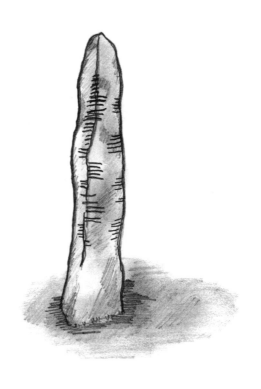

## Ogham

Pronounced 'ohm', ogham is an ancient Irish system of writing. Made up of groups of parallel straight or slanting lines cut on either side of a central divider, it is found carved into hundreds of stones around Ireland. Ogham also used to be written on sticks, though none of these have survived.

### *Poitín*

*Poitín* (pronounced 'putch-een', literally 'little pot') is a strong spirit alcohol, traditionally made in a small pot still. It was illegal for hundreds of years, made in secret on remote hillsides. Usually made from malted barley, it can also be distilled from other cereals, sugar beet, molasses or potatoes.

## Province: Connacht

Ireland is made up of four provinces, and Connacht comprises five western counties: Galway, Leitrim, Mayo, Roscommon and Sligo. When Irish Catholics were driven off their lands during the Cromwellian conquest in the 1600s, they were told they could go 'to Hell or Connacht', as although a spectacularly beautiful place, the province's land is mostly fairly poor, being largely rocky and boggy.

## Province: Leinster

Positioned on the eastern side of Ireland, Leinster is the most populous province of the island. It consists of twelve counties, including Dublin, and is home to nearly 3 million people. This is where the Vikings first arrived in Ireland, as well as the Normans.

## Province: Munster

Munster is the southwestern corner of the country, comprising counties Clare, Cork, Kerry, Limerick, Tipperary and Waterford. It is noted for Gaelic games, traditional music, Gaeltacht areas and the natural poetic inclinations of its people. Its biggest city is Cork, the second-largest city in Ireland.

## Province: Ulster

The northern part of Ireland, Ulster includes the six counties of Northern Ireland and the three border counties of Cavan, Donegal and Monaghan. It was the last corner of Ireland to fall to the British occupation. The 'red hand' symbol was originally the family crest of the O'Neills, one of the great Gaelic clans.

## Pub

Irish pubs can be found in every corner
of the world, and are usually the best
pubs in those corners, but naturally
the very best Irish pubs are in Ireland.
A cosy haven for a fireside chat or
a raucous celebration, an Irish pub
boasts a unique ambience that greatly
enhances the flavour of a 'pint of plain'
or a 'ball of malt'.

### *Púca*

The *púca*, or pooka, is a fairy or ghost usually seen in the shape of a goat, though sometimes as a human with animal features, such as a tail or goat's ears. They can bring either good or bad luck, and it was once traditional to leave part of the harvest to placate the *púca*.

## Rain

If it didn't rain so much in Ireland, we would surely run out of things to talk about. It's what makes the country so green, makes the spuds grow and keeps the bogs good and boggy. There are many types of rain, from a 'grand soft day' to buckets of it hammering down sideways.

## The Rose of Tralee

Named after an eighteenth-century ballad about a lovely girl called Mary, The Rose of Tralee is an international beauty pageant and festival, on the go since 1959. Originally only for women from Tralee, it expanded to women from anywhere in Kerry, then all of Ireland and finally to any woman worldwide who can claim Irish ancestry, so long as she is 'lovely and fair as the rose of the summer'.

## Round tower

Usually found beside monasteries and large churches, Ireland's round towers date from the ninth to the twelfth centuries. Up to 130 feet (40 metres) tall, they had a door that was usually between 6 and 10 feet (2 or 3 metres) up from the ground and would have been accessed by ladder. As the Irish name *cloigtheach*, or 'bell house', suggests, they were built as belfries.

## St Brigid

One of Ireland's three patron saints, the others being St Patrick and St Columba, Brigid was born around AD 450 in County Louth. She spent her early years cooking and cleaning, then became a nun and went on to found many convents and churches.

St Brigid's crosses are woven out of rushes by thousands of schoolchildren on St Brigid's Day, 1 February, the Celtic first day of spring.

## St Patrick

Born in the late fourth century, Patrick was kidnapped by pirates aged around sixteen and sold as a slave in County Antrim. Eventually escaping, he felt he was called in a dream to teach the Irish about the Christian God. Twelve years later, he returned as a priest and travelled all over Ireland, establishing churches and baptising people. St Patrick's Day, 17 March, is celebrated worldwide with parades and the 'greening' of famous landmarks.

### *Sean nós* singing

Literally 'old style', *sean nós* songs
are sung unaccompanied, usually in
a highly ornamented style. A *sean
nós* singer often clasps the hand of a
nearby listener, 'winding' the song out.
The songs can be laments, love songs,
historical songs about rebellions or
famine, or comic songs, often involving
alcohol. *Sean nós* is traditionally
learned by ear.

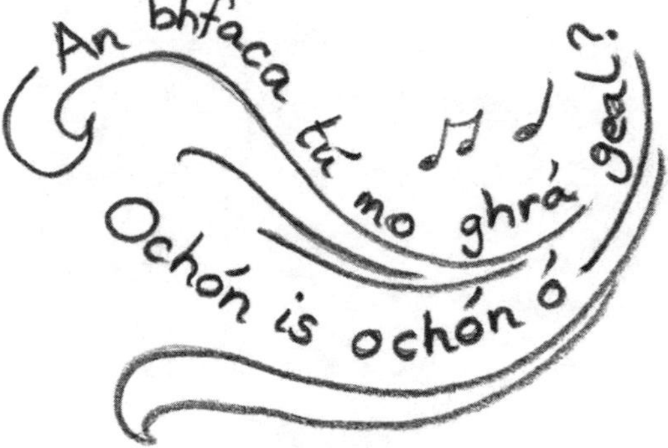
An bhfaca tú mo ghrá geal?
Ochón is ochón ó

## Shamrock

St Patrick used a shamrock to explain the mystery of the Christian Holy Trinity to the pagan Irish: three leaves and one stem – father, son and holy spirit, all part of one God. Ever since, we all wear a bit of shamrock on St Patrick's Day, to explain that we've had only one pint when we actually had three.

## Sheela na gig

A Sheela na gig, or *Síle na gig*, is a type of Irish gargoyle in the shape of a woman with a large, skull-like head, her hands holding open an exaggerated vulva. From the eleventh century on, they were often placed on churches, though their origin is much earlier. It is unclear whether they represent fertility or were perhaps a supernatural aid to childbirth.

### Shillelagh

A shillelagh (pronounced 'shill-ay-lee') is a stout walking stick or cudgel, usually made from a blackthorn stick, with a large knob on the end. It was traditionally smeared with butter or fat and placed up the chimney to cure, then painted with black paint or magpie's blood.

### *Sídhe*

The *sídhe* (pronounce 'shee') are Ireland's fairy folk, the 'little people'. They are descended from the Tuatha Dé Danann, who populated Ireland before the coming of the Milesians and then the Celts. Slim and handsome, they are great musicians and poets. They take many forms, from harmless enough leprechauns and sprites to malign spirits like the *dúlachan*, a headless rider whose wagon is covered with dried human skin.

## Skellig Islands

Twelve kilometres from the Kerry coast,
Skellig Michael and Little Skellig are
jagged and forbidding rocks, pounded
relentlessly by North Atlantic storms.
Skellig Michael is best known for
the 'beehive' huts of St Fionán's
monastic community, who scratched
out an austere living here in
early Christian times.
George Bernard Shaw called it *'the
most fantastic and impossible rock in
the world … part of our dream world.'*

## Soda bread

The 'soda' in soda bread is the raising agent sodium bicarbonate, or 'baking soda', used instead of yeast. The other basic ingredients are flour, salt and buttermilk. It is especially delicious hot from the oven, with a generous slather of farmhouse butter and some fresh jam.

### Spuds

The worst tragedy that ever struck Ireland was the Great Famine, or Great Hunger, of the 1840s, when the potato crop that poor tenant farmers relied on as their staple food fell victim to blight. The British occupying forces did little to lessen their suffering. One million people died, and another million emigrated. You can see why we still value our spuds!

## Stone circle

In some remote parts of the country, usually on an elevated hillside, can be found large standing stones arranged in a circle. At many stone circles, the rising or setting sun at one of the solstices or equinoxes lines up with two large entrance stones. They seem to have had some sort of ceremonial or religious purpose.

## Tara brooch

One of Ireland's greatest national treasures, this large brooch was found near the seashore in County Meath in 1850. It is exquisitely decorated with gold filigree in animal and abstract patterns, with scrolls, triple spirals and La Tène motifs. Dating from the eighth century AD, it is a truly extraordinary example of artisan work of the time.

## Thatched cottage

The Irish thatched cottage is traditionally built of local stone, covered with lime mortar or mud plaster and whitewashed. It usually has small windows and a 'half-door' that can open in two halves. Often consisting of just one room, these cottages housed large families, and often the pigs and chickens would live here too!

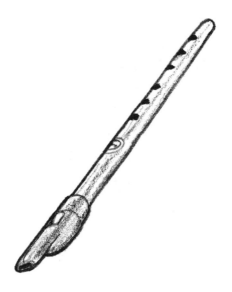

### Tin whistle

The tin whistle, or *feadóg*, has six holes and can play a diatonic scale over two octaves. It is taught in primary schools throughout the country, primarily for traditional music. Though a very simple instrument, very advanced melodies can be played on it.

## Tree of life

For the Celts, trees represented
strength and wisdom, as well as rebirth.
The Celtic tree of life, or *crann bethadh*,
is a very ancient symbol, representing
the balance and interconnectedness
of nature. The roots reach into the
Underworld, and the branches reach
into the Heavens, connecting both
to the Earth.

## Tricolour

Many countries have tricolour flags, but Ireland's has the nicest colours – green, representing the nationalist population; orange, which stands for the northern unionist people; and white in the middle, representing peace between the two traditions. Raised over the GPO in Dublin during the 1916 Easter Rising, it was officially adopted as our national flag when we gained independence in 1922.

## Trinity knot

This is a knotwork motif found in ancient gospels, in church windows and many other places. It can be single or double, and sometimes has a circle interlocked with it. In Christian contexts, it is thought to represent the Holy Trinity. It is much older than Christianity, though, and its original meaning is unknown.

### Triskel

Nobody is entirely sure what the triskel, another very ancient Irish symbol, represents. It could be mind-body-spirit, or birth-life-death, or past-present-future – or maybe it is the symbol for a stone-age tricycle. It is found carved into rock at ancient sites such as Newgrange in County Meath.

### Turf

With our many damp boglands, for centuries turf was the main fuel for the people of Ireland. Cut with a *sleán*, a sort of two-sided spade, the turf had to be stacked to dry, and then restacked to dry some more. Cutting turf is hard, physical work, but the smell of a real turf fire is incomparable.

## Uilleann pipes

Uilleann, or elbow, pipes are a fairly complicated musical instrument made of blackwood, leather, bamboo, copper, silver, brass and bone. A bellows under the right arm inflates a leather bag under the left. This is squeezed, feeding air to the chanter, which plays the melody, and the regulators, which make a drone or can be used to play chords.

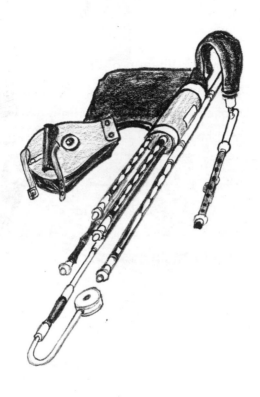

## Wake

This is how we mark the passing of a loved one in Ireland. A wake is held before the funeral, usually in the home of the deceased, with that person laid out so that visitors can say farewell. Involving prayer, consolation, reminiscence, drink, song and laughter, it goes on well into the night, or sometimes two or three nights. Many cups of tea and glasses of whiskey are raised in honour of the departed.

## Whiskey

Whiskey was invented by the Irish, and the word comes from the Irish *uisce beatha*, meaning 'water of life'. Made of malted and unmalted barley, it is usually distilled three times in a copper pot still. Regulations state that it must be aged for at least three years in oak barrels.

## Wren boys

The twenty-sixth of December is wren day, or *lá an dreoilín* in Irish.

In a tradition still carried on in parts of the west, 'wren boys', also known as 'mummers', dress in costumes made of straw and all manner of other bizarre clothing and go around the locality, playing music, dancing and collecting donations of money and alcohol.

Stately, plump B
came f
a

## Writers

Ireland has produced many of the world's greatest writers, including Beckett, Behan, Binchy, Bowen, Edgeworth, Friel, Gregory, Heaney, Joyce, Kavanagh, Kinsella, a couple of O'Briens, O'Casey, Russell, Shaw, Stoker, Swift, Synge, Wilde, Yeats … Is it the wicked Irish sense of humour? As Yeats put it, 'Being Irish, he had an abiding sense of tragedy, which sustained him through temporary periods of joy.'

**Eoin O'Brien** has all the luck of the Irish. He loves to write and draw, and sing songs and play music. He lives with an amazing wife and two beautiful children in a house full of guitars.